RICK'S JOKE OF BOOKS II

A Second Collection of Rick's Lousy Jokes Spanning Decades

PLEASE

**No singing
No dancing
No swearing**

This is a respectable joke book

RICK'S JOKE OF BOOKS II

A Second Collection of Rick's Lousy Jokes Spanning Decades

By
RICK

BOOKSTAND
·PUBLISHING·
ESTD. 2006

www.bookstandpublishing.com

Published by
Bookstand Publishing
Pasadena, CA 91101
4977_1

Copyright © 2024 by Rick Helley
All rights reserved. No part of this publication may be reproduced or transmitted in any form or by any means, electronic or mechanical, including photocopy, recording, or any information storage and retrieval system, without permission in writing from the copyright owner.
(Note: This Copyright does not extend to the names of Trademarked characters and products mentioned herein, which are the properties of their respective owners, or to the front cover/divider page photo, which is from iStock.)

Cover Designed and Prepared by Al Margolis.

ISBN 978-1-956785-77-7

DEDICATIONS

To my parents, **Louise** and **Richard Helley**, my brother, **Bill Williams**, my grandmother, **Harriet Andersen**, and my dog, **Snooper**. Thank you for being the most wonderful family with which I could have possibly been blessed. I truly love you and miss you all so much.

To **Don Rickles**, **Tim Conway**, **Jackie Gleason**, **The Three Stooges** (all six), and, most of all, **Laurel & Hardy**, for blessing me with decades of laughter and the world with your wonderful legacies of timeless comedy.

To **Emily Veeh**, Boss Lady extraordinaire, for making this and my first joke book possible.

To **Mrs. Rae**, **Mrs. Adams**, **Mrs. Hinton**, **Mrs. Cronk**, **Mr. Hunter**, and **Professor Pann**, the finest schoolteachers I ever had.

To **Rosalyn (Lyn) Moran**, former Associate Editor of *International GYMNAST* magazine, who gave me my start as a published author in 1977.

To **Wally Gibson** and **Steve Dawson**, who showed me how much magic, fun, comedy, and mystery there is in a deck of cards and a handful of coins.

To **Brooks D. Kubik**, the Original Dinosaur, who brought back Old School Training.

And finally:

To **Mrs. Sigglekow**, **Mrs. Edmonston**, and **Mrs. Schneider** — wherever you are.

DISCLAIMER
(And Dat Claimer)

The names of Trademarked characters and products mentioned herein are used strictly per and for Nominative Fair Use purposes, and are entirely the properties of the respective owners, Trademark holders, and rights-holders of those characters and products.

None of the persons, places, or things mentioned herein, Trademarked or otherwise, constitute endorsements of this book or its contents by said entities or their owners.

Also, please note that AI (Addle-brained Idiocy) played a significant role in the writing of both this book and its predecessor.

FOREWORD

By Fortunato

Ugh! ugh! ugh!—ugh! ugh! ugh!—
ugh! ugh! ugh!—ugh! ugh! ugh!—
ugh! ugh! ugh!

CONTENTS

(UNDER PRESSURE. DO NOT PUNCTURE OR INCINERATE.)

DEDICATIONS v

DISCLAIMER
   (AND DAT CLAIMER) vii

FOREWORD
   BY FORTUNATO viii

INTRODUCTION x

THE LOUSY JOKES 3

MORE LOUSY STUFF 121

APPENDIX: TESTIMOANIALS
   AND PREYS FROM READERS 137

ABOUT RICK (WHO HE?) 141

INTRODUCTION

The book you're now holding (and may soon be casting into your wastebasket but hopefully not), *RICK'S JOKE OF BOOKS II*, is the follow-on to my highly unsuccessful first joke book, *RICK'S JOKE OF BOOKS*. As such, the present volume contains those lousy jokes that didn't make it into the first book, because either I had failed to remember them while writing that book, or I remembered them only after the first book was already in print.

As with my first book, please note that, unlike some other joke books, the jokes herein are not neatly organized under various categories, e.g., Buttercream Flowers, Drag Racing, Monkeypox, OTC Non-steroid Anti-inflammatories, Tai Chi, Vintage Dumbbells, etc. Instead, they appear here pretty much as a random streamof-consciousness agglomeration, typed in pretty much as they popped into my head. This is not due to laziness on my part. It's because, I'm ashamed to admit, I was never able to understand, much less master, the Dewey Decimal Lousy Joke Classification System (DDLJCS), one of my great failings in life. (Actually it IS due to laziness on my part, but I'm trying to save at least a little face here.)

But willy-nilly as the contents herein may be, I do hope there's enough variety among the jokes to at least mildly amuse people of many diverse tastes and interests (including Monkeypox aficionados).

Enjoy! (Or not, as the case may be.)

But in any event, thanks for at least giving this book a chance.

—Rick Helley
October 22, 2024

"To truly laugh, you must be able to take your pain and play with it."

— Charlie Chaplin

"Life is SO difficult — everybody's been through something! But you laugh at it, it becomes smaller."

— Joan Rivers

RICK'S JOKE OF BOOKS II

CAUTION
HEAVY READING AHEAD

By RICK

RICK'S JOKE OF BOOKS II

THE
LOUSY JOKES

By RICK

RICK'S JOKE OF BOOKS II

This book starts off slowly, but then it tapers off.

Q: What do rabbits do after they get married?
A: They go on their bunnymoon.

Drag racing dragged out can be a real drag.

Is the Monkeypox outbreak just a rumor or a gibbon?

Other than a sudden urge to scarf down bananas and swing on vines, I've noted no ill effects or symptoms from Monkeypox.

"Golf" spelled backwards is "Flog."

By RICK

Nuclear weapons may ensure that all people are cremated equal.

Moving to the U.S., Tarzan took up residence in a swing state.

The pirate became an opera singer, and in time became well-known for his stirring Arr-Arr-Arias.

GUY: "Is my hairline receding?"
FRIEND: "Turn around. Yep, it sure is."

Gazing with amazement at the complete, perfectly preserved skeleton of the Cro-Magnon Man, the archaeologist gushed, "Absolutely cro-magnificent!"

RICK'S JOKE OF BOOKS II

After eating five cans of alphabet soup at one sitting, he had the sudden urge to move his vowels. Fortunately, he wasn't consonantpated.

The church pastor took to using hand-puppets during his Sunday sermons to emphasize key points. Uncertain at first over the pastor's unconventional preaching technique, the congregation members soon came to enjoy his pulpit shows.

His book on the history of cannons became yet another title added to the cannon canon.

For yogis, financial problems can be a pain in the asana.

By RICK

Q: What's the favorite meat of dress designers?
A: Skirt Steak.

Q: If hot pants catch fire, how do you extinguish the flames?
A: With the pantyhose.

Requiring major surgery to remove part of his colon, the grammarian was left with a semicolon.

Losing his prized pair of vintage collectible loaded dice, the crooked gambler related his tale of woe in his memoir, *Pair of Dice Lost*.

As the newly married insects stepped out of the church, the guests showered them with lice.

RICK'S JOKE OF BOOKS II

As a little kid reciting The Pledge of Allegiance each morning in elementary school in the 1960s, I always wondered what kind of drink Liver Tea was. (In my mind's eye, I'd always see men in white powdered wigs drinking cups of grey-brown liquid.)

Singing "Jingle Bells" in the first grade in the early 1960s, I could never figure out what a One Hore Soapen Sleigh was.

The firefighters successfully rescued the prostitutes from their burning brothel, but such required the use of their Hooker Ladder Truck.

By RICK

Dermatologists have a lot of skin in the game.

Q: What's the favorite digital currency among super-heroes with powers and abilities far beyond those of ordinary mortals?
A: Krypto currency.

The baker was making little money, and his expenses were piling up, so he really kneaded the dough.

I'm so old that I remember The Fall of the Roman Empire. I wasn't actually there to witness it in person. But I do distinctly remember hearing a huge CRASH right around that time.

RICK'S JOKE OF BOOKS II

HORSE TO COWBOY: "Get off my back!"

The skunk was so poor that all it had was a scent.

Q: How do you recognize a Dogwood Tree?
A: By its bark.

Q: What do you call two elephants contending for the World Heavyweight Championship, with 10-ounce gloves affixed to their noses?
A: Boxing trunks.

Carpet Diem: Seize the Rug!

The favorite college course of skeletons: Bonehead English.

By RICK

Q: What's the favorite classic cinematic sword-and-sorcery epic among entomologists?
A: *Jason and the Golden Fleas*.

Q: What's the favorite classic cinematic sword-and-sorcery epic among dentists?
A: *Jason and the Golden Floss*.

Divorced Sea Anemones must sometimes pay court-ordered Sea Alimony.

Retiring from her career as a figure skater, she enrolled in and finished law school, passed the Bar Exam, and became a Slip-and-Slide lawyer.

A high-quality chimney can cost enough to brick the bank.

RICK'S JOKE OF BOOKS II

If the plural of Octopus is Octopi, then the plural of Platypus should be Platypi.

It's little known that Davy Crockett survived the siege of the Alamo, developed an interest in rocketry, and became the world's first Crockett scientist.

Following his bitter divorce, Davy Crockett was forced to pay Alamony.

Sea Anemones must keep warm during the cold winter months in order to lessen their chances of contracting Sea Anemonia.

A long-time tractor company employee, she sent her boyfriend a John Deere® letter.

By RICK

The well-equipped brothel includes faucets fitted with water philtres.

In order to graduate from bartending school, student bartenders must pass the Bar Exam.

In order to qualify for sewer maintenance jobs, candidates must obtain the proper crud-dentials.

What is it with so many websites? They request my Cookie Preferences, but never give me any options, e.g., Oatmeal Raisin, Chocolate Chip, Peanut Butter, or even Snickerdoodle.

He went from selling Plaster of Paris to being plastered in Paris.

RICK'S JOKE OF BOOKS II

Adolf Hitler was one tough cookie, his actual name being Adolf Snickerdoodle.

Q: What's the favorite dairy product among practitioners of the Chinese internal healing and martial arts?
A: Tai Cheese.

The blind mathematician communicated with sine language.

Q: What's the most famous and popular rock band among insects?
A: The Dung Beatles.

Actually served at my high school in the early 1970s: Imitation Ice Milk.

By RICK

The key to living to 80 is to not pass away at 79.

Q: Where do married puppets with troubled relationships go for counseling?
A: To marionette counselors.

Q: What's the favorite dairy product among marionettes?
A: String Cheese.

As a side-hustle, Santa entered the soft-drink cola-producing industry, advertising his cola with the slogan "The Claus that Refreshes."

The witch was a beach bum, known as the Sand Witch.

RICK'S JOKE OF BOOKS II

The witch was crabby and ill-tempered, at the slightest provocation flying off the handle.

As a little girl, the witch liked running around the house, pretending her toy broom was a race car, and shouting "Brooom! Brooom!"

Q: What's the best food to barbecue on October 31st?
A: Halloweenies.

Obtaining his amateur radio license, the pig became a Ham Operator.

Passing the Bar Exam, the skeleton became a *Pro Bono* attorney.

By RICK

A member of Skull & Bones, the Bonesman could open any door using his skeleton key.

Secret society for book formatters: The Knights-Template.

Secret society for comedians: The Illuminutty.

Well-known are the Freemasons. Little-known are the Captivemasons.

Under harsh interrogation by the authorities, the high-ranking Freemason was subjected to the Thirty-Third Degree.

Known as "The Charming Gymnast," she loved performing Mega Rolls.

RICK'S JOKE OF BOOKS II

Q: What are the favorite meats among practitioners of the Japanese martial arts?
A: Judo Chops and Karate Chops.

Q: What's the favorite self-defense technique of pigs?
A: Pork Chops.

Q: What are the favorite self-defense techniques of sheep?
A: Lamb Chops and Mutton Chops.

Q: What's the favorite cleaning liquid in the Sea Anemone community?
A: Sea Anemmonia.

Kachina Ka-Ching Ka-Ching dolls are rare and very expensive.

By RICK

As a side-hustle, the Gibbon took up shoe-shining. Unfortunately, it didn't work out, as the public wouldn't stand for any monkeyshines.

I'm really enjoying the new science fiction TV series *Dog Trek*, featuring the space travel adventures of Captain Cur, his Vulcanine Science Officer, his Chief Medical Officer Bones, his Scottish Terrier Chief Engineer, and his Security Officer Mr. Woof.

Grass-fed beef cattle are used to produce potted meat.

Vincent van Gogh's lesser-known artist cousin: van Stopp.

RICK'S JOKE OF BOOKS II

What I always tell any friend who's about to undergo surgery: "Just don't Take a Turn for the Nurse, and you'll be fine."

Some rodeo cowboys have Bucket Bronco Lists.

Before Franciscan friar William of Occam ventured into philosophy, he was an innovative fence designer, famous for having invented Occam's Razor Wire.

Living far out in the wilderness, the woodsman became known as Daniel Boondocks.

My Bucket List pails in comparison to most others.

By RICK

The harrowing story of the grape who gradually transformed into a raisin is told in the classic novel, *The Picture of Dorian Grape*.

John Steinbeck and Gene Roddenberry joined forces to write and produce the classic science fiction film, *The Grapes of Wrath of Khan*.

Maybe someday I'll be able to order a Chai Tea in a Starbucks™ without saying "Tai Chi."

Q: How do caterpillars greet one another on December 25th?
A: "Merry Chrysalis!"

A rabbit's foot is a good luck charm — except for the rabbit.

RICK'S JOKE OF BOOKS II

It could rightly be said that a porta-potty maintenance truck is a kind of dump truck.

When one door closes behind you, another door slams shut in your face.

For your own safety, never tell an Amazon, even in jest, that she looks like an online bookstore, or ask her where her shopping cart is. Amazons have no sense of humor, and you might get the stuffing beaten out of you.

Old doctors never die, they just lose all their patience.

I'm enjoying reruns of that great 1950s TV sitcom about a successful gambler, *I Love Lucky*.

By RICK

Old golfers never die, they just get more strokes.

If Charles Atlas had taken a different career path and had become a mail order writing instructor: "Wow! It didn't take Charles Atlas long to do this for me! What GRAMMAR! What PUNCTUATION! That editor won't Red-pen ME around again!"

An advertising sign I saw posted prominently outside a store many years ago: "SNAIL PELLETS 49 CENTS." I'm sure that attracted a veritable stampede of customers.

FBI = Fat, Bald and Ignorant.

RICK'S JOKE OF BOOKS II

The U.N. = The Untied Nations.

An unfortunate side effect of his Lobotomy was major depression, such that whenever he looked in the mirror he muttered morosely, "Low Bottom Me."

Q: What's the favorite core exercise of pirates?
A: Walking the Plank.

Q: What do you get when you cross Mr. Green Jeans™ with Green Lantern™?
A: Mr. Green Lantern-Jeans.

Q: What's the favorite chest exercise in the Oval Office?
A: The Bench Prez.

By RICK

Katydids flourished, but Katydidn'ts didn't.

Q: What do you get when you cross The Flash™ with a sailboat?
A: A Flash Sail.

Q: What was the favorite 1960s spy television show among chiropractors?
A: *I Spine*.

I was married once. And what an hour THAT was.

I'm not a corn-fed man; I'm a cornball man.

Am I the only person who at first glance mistakes "CPAP" for "CRAP"?

RICK'S JOKE OF BOOKS II

While the proposed 1960s science fiction TV series about a space-faring garbage scow picking up litter throughout the known Universe in the 23rd Century sounded intriguing, none of the networks were interested in airing *Star Dreck*.

Nor were the networks back then interested in the proposed science fiction series about space-faring bodybuilders pumping up their biceps while exploring the (Mr.) Universe, *Star Pec*.

Sludge Lagoon, the heroic pirate, carried so many stout barmaids from the burning pub to safety that he wenched his lower back.

By RICK

No sooner had his shingles healed when he broke out in Spanish roofing tiles and got the shakes.

The unmarried roofing contractor joined an online dating service for shingles.

He much preferred currying his horse to reading philosophy, always putting the horse before Descartes.

Taking a leisurely stroll, the caveman and cave woman just neandered along.

Q: What's the preferred sedative used in the Papacy?
A: Ativatican.

RICK'S JOKE OF BOOKS II

Looking as if she'd been poured into the "little black dress" that was several sizes too small, she prided herself on being an early adopter of the latest style trend, the Hooker Rhinoceros Look.

DENTIST: "I'm terribly sorry! The drill just slipped right out of my hand! Are you all right?"
PATIENT: "I'm good. But I think your chair was damaged when the drill bored through the back of my head."

Profanity is bad, but amateurfanity is even worse.

There's a new generic for Prozac®: Amateurzac.

By RICK

After slaying a Tyrannosaurus Rex, John Wilkes Booth's remote ancestor was heard to shout, "Sic Semper Tyrannosaurus!"

On trial for punching a smiling fortune teller, the defendant claimed he was merely striking a happy medium.

Q: How can you identify happy motorcycle riders?
A: By the bugs on their teeth.

Corned beef hash AGAIN! Pinch me! I must be living a DREAM!

At the conclusion of the breakfast cereal magnate's wedding, the guests threw puffed rice.

RICK'S JOKE OF BOOKS II

Snakes with Hay Fever are raving about the latest class of OTC anti-allergy drugs designed just for them — Anti-Hissstamines.

In a top secret scientific experiment, Captain Kangaroo™ and Captain Crunch™ were merged into a single person, Captain Cruncharoo.

All of us human beings have but a short dance in the sun in this world. And it ends with "Taps."

Alas, my life in this world is but a short dance in the sun. Oops! I Bucked when I should've Winged!

"Shipping Label Created" does NOT mean the item has shipped.

By RICK

Dedicating his life to promoting dolphin-safe tuna, he led a porpoise-driven life.

Purchasing a foundering refrigerator manufacturing company, he turned it around and became a successful refrigerator magnate.

Living a boring life in a boring sea, the octopus couldn't find anything interesting to octopi his time.

Have you heard the one about the ghosts who compiled Kicked-the-Bucket Lists? Well now you have!

I'm in luck! Bedlam has a spare bed!

My stewed tomatoes need black coffee.

RICK'S JOKE OF BOOKS II

Long-abandoned Alcatraz Island has been proposed as the site for a new amusement park — Prisneyland.

As a drop-dead-gorgeous gold-digger who had cleverly and expertly attracted and burned through several elderly wealthy husbands who left her uber-rich after they kicked the bucket, she was a highly polished trophy wife.

I'm such lousy husband material that I've never even merited a participation trophy wife.

Taking up exercise to improve their health, The Three Stooges™ became avid dumbbell trainees.

By RICK

Some years ago, Killer Bees were big in the news. At the time, I imagined them to be attired in double-breasted suits and hats, wielding Tommy guns, and flying up to people and growling, "Okay, Rosebud, dis is a STICK-UP! It's yer honey or yer life!"

Sage advice for cowboy weightlifters: Never squat with your spurs on.

They've added Break-dancing to the Olympics as of this writing (2024). So what's next? Olympic Hopscotch? Olympic Poker? Olympic Couch-Potatoing? Olympic Watching The Old Paint Peeling Off A Barn? (I could win a Gold Medal in the latter.)

RICK'S JOKE OF BOOKS II

Walking face-first into a floor lamp, his nose swelled up and became bulbous.

Some scientists claim that Time doesn't exist. My face in the mirror and my aching arthritic joints beg to differ.

Although "Nuptials" is a synonym for "wedding ceremony," I think the word sounds a lot more like the name of a finger food, a snack food, or small candies.

Bananas are useless. Throw away the peel, and that big white bone inside, and there's nothing left to eat.

By RICK

Q: What dinosaur had the largest muscular arms?
A: The Tricepatops.

Q: What's the world's rarest and most valuable animal?
A: The Duck-Billed Platinumpus.

"Brrr! It's the middle of Summer — and it's...it's...FREEZING!"
"See? I told you that Global Warming is real."

The hideous witch fancied herself being as beautiful as Helen of Troy, when in reality she had The Face That Launched A Thousand Sh*ts.

The bird flew up through a flue not knowing it was carrying the bird flu.

RICK'S JOKE OF BOOKS II

To build up their muscles and strength for battle, Achilles and Hector lifted Troy weights.

Running afoul of the law, the Yoga instructor was in deep yogurt.

In the next Summer Olympics a new sport will be introduced specifically for disagreeable, unpleasant, and ill-tempered people: Gymnasties.

Q: What was the headache doctor's favorite breakfast cereal?
A: My Grain.

The poor cat lost a forepaw in a lawnmower accident, the whole situation an unfortunate faux pas.

The drunken comedian was a ham on rye.

By RICK

Slacking off in his job, he went from being a skilled interior decorator to an inferior decorator.

Hailing from The Red Planet, he was a master of the Martian arts.

He fancied himself a super-villain, the arch-nemesis of all super-heroes. However, it was all in his mind, for in reality he was but a faux foe.

As notorious pirate poet Robert The Frost once wrote: "Good wenches make good neighbors."

Your undertaker: The last friend to let you down.

RICK'S JOKE OF BOOKS II

I've heard of Life Coaches — but *Dating Coaches*? I mean, really? Do they offer their clients refunds if dates go south?

A waffle lover, Sigmund Freud originated and published his theory of the Eggo and the Super-Eggo.

Friar Tuck became an expert in cooking French Fries, thus becoming known as French Friar Tuck.

It's little known that Hitler's paramour and briefly his wife, Eva Braun, had a sister who loved potatoes for breakfast and Corned Beef Hash for dinner. Her name, long lost to history until recently, was Hash Braun.

By RICK

The window installer picked up the heavy window incorrectly, thus injuring his lower back and ending up with severe back pane.

Long before the arrival of Quantum Physics, a Native American scientist developed Wampum Physics.

With the right resources and tools, good schoolteachers can repair lots of dense.

FOOD WRITER: "What are your favorite vegetables?"
MAN ON THE STREET: "Potato chips and French Fries."

An accomplished glider pilot, the T-Rex was a skilled dinosoar.

RICK'S JOKE OF BOOKS II

Q: How can you tell if an elephant's raided your refrigerator?
A: By the footprints in the pizza.

All I remember from my college Psychology class in 1975 is "Corpus Callosum." What I don't remember is how far it is from Corpus Christi.

Q: Among retired brain surgeons, what's the favorite city to move to and reside in?
A: Corpus Callosum Christi.

He kissed like a vacuum cleaner; his kisses really sucked.

Having one ugly mug, I'm not everyone's cup of tea.

By RICK

The bald man thought that Liver Pâté was a toupee adhesive. Unfortunately, his using it as such rendered his toupee rather the wurst for wear.

Q: What classic amusement park ride is constructed entirely of iron?
A: The Ferrous Wheel.

A skilled artist, the phlebotomist drew a pen-and-ink rendition of Noah's Ark on raging waters. Art critics acclaimed the work as a superb flood draw.

Mourning Doves and Morning Glories, or Morning Doves and Mourning Glories? I'm so confused.

RICK'S JOKE OF BOOKS II

A non-starter: DIY Brain Surgery.

In life, the chef specialized in Haute Cuisine; after he passed away, his ghost specialized in Haunt Cuisine.

Fusion Cooking with seafood ingredients: Fission Cooking.

Misplacing the prized cookbooks he relied upon, the chef had no choice but to resort to Confusion Cooking.

Through its clandestine uranium enrichment program to produce nuclear weapons, the rogue nation was engaged in centrifuge subterfuge.

By RICK

The disorganized, haphazard Nuclear Fusion research program devolved into a Nuclear Confusion program. Still, the scientists involved tried fission for compliments among their peers.

Whenever a woman says to a man, "Oh, you're so funny! You are SO funny!" what she really means is, "This guy's a weirdo and I wish I was anywhere else in the world but here with him." (Trust me on this.)

That which kills you doesn't make you stronger.

Upon his passing, he left no legacy, much less an armacy.

RICK'S JOKE OF BOOKS II

LIFE HACK FOR MEN:
If a woman asks you to perform a task, and you do so and she thanks you, never reply, "No problem. Sometimes these things just require a man's touch." However, you might get away with responding, in a deep bass voice, "My pleasure, Miss Lane," or, "It's all in a day's work for — Wonder Man."

Successfully naming all 88 constellations from memory, the young Astronomy prodigy was awarded a Constellation Prize.

Entering the illicit Black Market trade in fake high-end brand-name women's cosmetics, he became a rouge rogue.

By RICK

Steeped in Silver Age super-hero comic books as a kid, I dreamed of becoming a super-being with powers and abilities far beyond those of mortal men. Sadly, I never achieved that dream. However, I did at least become a stupor-being.

Changing careers from tooth-collecting to horseshoeing, the Tooth Fairy became the Tooth Farrier.

Strange thought I had upon awakening one morning: "Don't mess with me! I've got a Black Belt in Figure Skating!"

A master of fish cooking and kung-fu, he was a seafood sifu.

RICK'S JOKE OF BOOKS II

According to a recent e-mail I received, I can save up to 35% on Riviera Leather! Great! (What's Riviera Leather?)

Since they have dental implants, do they also have new-brain implants? Not asking for a friend.

"Fill 'er up with Ethyl and put it on my charge plate." (Ancient language unknown to the younger generations.)

Q: Seated at his desk in the Oval Office, what did the President of the United States say when the herd of elephants tromped in?
A: "I wasn't expecting you until tomorrow."

By RICK

Becoming a gambling addict with absolutely no talent for the craft, the Loch Ness monster lost tons of money and became known as the Luck-Less Monster.

Later, graduating from college with a Masters degree in Aeronautical Engineering, the Loch Ness Monster found gainful employment as the Loch-Heed Monster.

"My sister married an Irishman."
"Oh really?"
"No, O'Reilly."

The world is his oyster, but he's allergic to seafood.

Pretentious? *Moi?*

RICK'S JOKE OF BOOKS II

...ared that his troublesome dress shoe was finally fixed, the church pastor strode out of the shoe repair shop, joyously singing, "It is well, it is well, with my sole!"

Taking up plumbing as an occupation, the pirate's girlfriend became a skilled Pipe Wench.

The intricate clockwork motions of the Universe were briefly disrupted when the alarm went off.

Amazon has issued me a 97-cent refund. Spending spree, here I come!

It's a great joke tonight, but will I respect it in the morning?

By RICK

I used to be a butcher. But that career came to a sudden end the day I backed into my meat grinder and got a little behind in my work. Not only that, unable to pay my medical bills, I ended up in arrears.

A FABULOUS MAGIC TRICK:
1. Ask a spectator their age.
2. Add 10 years to it.
3. That will be the spectator's age 10 years from now!

100% guaranteed to work every time!

Happy Star Wars Day! Live Long and Prosper!

Humpty Dumpty's brother became a hardboiled detective.

RICK'S JOKE OF BOOKS II

"I am NOT Holier than Thou! Now if you'll excuse me, I have to straighten my halo."

A compelling subtitle can increase the salability of any book. For example:

> HOW TO WATCH PAINT PEELING OFF AN OLD BARN
> A Fast-paced Non-stop
> Adrenaline-pumping
> Edge-of-your-seat
> Action-adventure Thriller
> and How-To Guide

My barber's driving me crazy. Every time he cuts my hair he keeps singing, "Bar-Bar-Bar! Bar-ber I-Am!"

[This joke intentionally blank.]

By RICK

HE: "Gee, honey, you make the most delicious sandwiches in the world!"
SHE: "That's not a sandwich, it's my WALLET, you silly goose!"

The gastroenterologist author learned that his book on Irritable Bowel Syndrome required both ISBN <u>and</u> IBS Numbers. The news was hard for him to digest.

She was the sunshine of my life. But I had to wear 50-SPF sunscreen whenever I was around her in order to avoid being burned.

The contaminated Bird Nest Soup caused a real flap.

Lamented the decrepit old cow, "I'm but a ruminant of my former self."

RICK'S JOKE OF BOOKS II

Following the lead of Federal Express® changing its delivery service's name to the more easily remembered and catchier FedEx®, the U.S. Postal Service® is thinking of changing its name to P-Off.

Q: Who was the conman who fell asleep for 20 years after drinking a glass of strange liquor?
A: Ripoff van Winkle.

Deciding that dealing in real estate would be more profitable than wrecking it, the fire-breathing monster obtained his real estate license and changed his name to Godzillow.

The favorite leg exercise of witch bodybuilders: Goblin Squats.

53

By RICK

Becoming an atheist, the fire-breathing monster's twin brother changed his name to Godlesszilla.

The spice merchant was known for his sage and thymely advice.

Following his success with *The Legend of Sleepy Hollow* and the character The Headless Horseman, author Washington Irving found much less success with his saga about a down-on-his-luck Viking baker, The Breadless Norseman.

The Mormon firefighters formed their own denomination, The Church of Ladder-day Saints.

Other than feeling lousy, I feel fine.

RICK'S JOKE OF BOOKS II

Q: What's the best church for Labrador Retrievers?
A: The Church of Labraday Saints.

Q: How do you greet a cosmetics saleswoman in The Czech Republic?
A: "Aloe, Vera."

Three sayings often uttered by my late father way back in the day: "He who steals my purse steals sh*t," "You know what I say? I say sh*t," and "Snug as a bug in a rug."

Answering my phone in a Popeye voice is, I've discovered, a great way to stun phone solicitors into complete silence.

In a parallel universe, lettuce is high-calorie while milk chocolate has zero calories.

By RICK

Q: What's the preferred vacation spot for ED doctors?
A: Viagra Falls.

Dear online retailers: Why on earth do I need an Automatic 3-month Refill for SOCKS? Nutritional supplements and OTC medications, I could understand. But SOCKS?

All I have to do is browse online for, say, sliced turkey, and thereafter images of sliced turkey packages pop up on every website I visit.

Dear phone solicitors: Let me save you some time. My Extended Car Warranty is fine, and, no, I'm not interested in selling my property.

RICK'S JOKE OF BOOKS II

Never a hit with the ladies, I was, instead, a miss with the Misses (and in my youth, the Missies).

Not only do the ladies never even give me the time of day, they won't even tell me what century this is.

My blood type being B-Positive, I've always regretted that I just missed an A-Minus.

Opening his own detective agency, Dick Tracy became a Private Dick.

Going against his church's doctrine, the pharmacist was accused of Apothecarytasy.

"Wealth Management" — Bwahh, Hah-Hah-Hah! Oh stop it! STOP it! You're KILLING me!

By RICK

After years of hard work, he realized his ambition of becoming a foam rubber magnate, his goal ever since his foamative years.

Iris was an apt pupil.

FATHER TO TEENAGED SON: "Stop saying you didn't ask to be born! For your information, your mother and I had an accident!"

There should be a nudist colony for seniors, i.e., an oldist colony.

I've discovered that my entire life is a simulation. The problem is that I keep saying "Computer, end program," but nothing ever happens.

RICK'S JOKE OF BOOKS II

Seeing the bug hit the windshield and get splattered, the driver shook his head and muttered sadly, "That bug won't have enough guts to do that again."

A new book on the history of airports is a runway best seller.

Glamorous on the outside but a shrew on the inside, she wasn't a trophy wife, but a trophy strife.

I just heard a rumor that author L. Sprague de Camp has de camped.

Q: What's the favorite type of Ouija Board among window washers?
A: The Squeegee Board.

By RICK

DRUNK #1: "Say, pal, izzat the sun or the moon up there?"
DRUNK #2: "I dunno, buddy. I'm new around here."

COLLEGE COED: "Dad, I'm thinking of changing my major from Mechanical Engineering to Philosophy."
FATHER: "Great idea. Then you'll be able to get a good job at that Philosophy factory they're planning on building downtown."

A sure sign you're a nobody is when no one ever even butt-dials you.

Accidentally swallowing a bar of soap, he ended up with the cleanest ulcer in town.

RICK'S JOKE OF BOOKS II

Last night I was shocked to observe a mob of chickens, all wearing white sheets and white hoods, descend upon my property and burn a big wooden wishbone on my front lawn. I just found out they're members of that notorious organization, a real chicken outfit, the Kluck Klucks Klan.

As my father used to say: "Tarzan, spelled backwards, Nazrat."

As my mother used to say: "Rin Tin Tin, spelled backwards, Nit Nit Nir."

On a parallel universe's earth, it's 3 O'Morn in the Clocking.

It took me 8 months to finish the jigsaw puzzle, but I was quite proud of myself because on the box it said "2 to 4 Years."

By RICK

Abandoning his career of writing horror stories in order to become a Hawaiian-foods chef, the 19th century Gothic fiction writer and poet changed his name to Edgar Allen Poi.

"Call me a cab."
"All right, you're a cab."

You know you're a flop as an author when you hold a book signing at a bookstore, and the only people lined up in front of your table are two stewed-to-the-gills winos who stumbled inside to get out of the cold.

I think it's ironic that, for many, Labor Day is a day off from labor.

RICK'S JOKE OF BOOKS II

Not a joke, per se, but I must include the oft-used phrase in a series of paperback Kung-Fu novels I enjoyed reading in the early 1970s: "And the goon was dead before he hit the floor."

Switching careers from sailor to construction worker, Barnacle Bill the Sailor changed his name to Particle Board the Nailer.

When Pandora opened Pandora's Box, things quickly went from the frying pan-dora into the fire.

A bald man going to a barber shop is the height of follicle.

A passionate fund-raiser, the baker enjoyed raisin bread.

By RICK

The Pit Stop Hair Removal Salon charges only a pittance for its services.

The hair removal salon owner was forced to retire early, after contracting a depilatating illness.

In my hometown, a new hair removal salon was opened, but then closed permanently the very next day. It was hair today, gone tomorrow.

I'm looking forward to that new television documentary, "A History of Hair Removal: The Depilatory Story."

Fifty years ago, "an Amazon order" would have meant something else.

RICK'S JOKE OF BOOKS II

Some scientists say that today's birds descended from the dinosaurs. That would explain the Tyrannosaurus Wren that's been terrorizing my neighborhood lately.

Q: What did Colonel Sanders say upon his retirement?
A: "I'll miss this chicken outfit."

Corn Silk was the most beautiful ear of corn in the entire corn field. Unfortunately, she was being obsessively stalked.

Said the martial arts master to the salacious film historian: "You have offended my family. And you have offended the Shirley Temple."

By RICK

The martial arts master took up gardening so that he could put plenty of Kung-Food on the table.

Q: Why do the elephants laugh at Tarzan?
A: They think his nose is funny.

"You're adroit."
"How DARE you call me a droit!"

The virologist became a major social media influenzer.

Foundering in agony on The Lake of Fire, he cried out in despair, "There's been a terrible mistake! I'm not supposed to be in Hell! I'm an American POLITICIAN!"

RICK'S JOKE OF BOOKS II

Q: What's the preferred dental restoration procedure among auto body shop workers?
A: Dented Implants.

The Chinese-restaurant owner received a quantity discount for ordering one ton of wontons.

His life shattered into pieces, Humpty Dumpty was but a shell of his former self.

Q: What does Humpty Dumpty NEVER order in a Chinese restaurant?
A: Egg Drop Soup.

Mison Mann was not very good at formulating best-laid plans.

By RICK

When you nod off in front of your computer, and you wake up with a start thinking it's Saturday when it's really Monday.

CAR SALESMAN: "This beauty's upholstered in Rich Corinthian Leather."
CUSTOMER: "I couldn't possibly afford it. Do you have one with Poor Corinthian Leather?"

Said by my father (jokingly) at his workplace: "Thank God it's Monday! I need the whole week to get my work done!"

He tells lots of little jokes — very little jokes.

The Gene Pool's in dire need of chlorine.

RICK'S JOKE OF BOOKS II

At my age I don't seize the day, I seize up in a daze.

LADY: "You're drunk."
DRUNK MAN: "Yer ugly."
LADY: "You are drunk."
DRUNK MAN: "Well at least I'll be sober in the mornin'."

The Abominable Snowman's favorite form of exercise: Icymetrics.

Bigfoot's favorite pasta: Spagh-Yeti.

"Alexa™, play the latest hit song for me."
"Alexeyev, clean and jerk 500 pounds."

Starting at the bottom, he liked it so he stayed there.

By RICK

The main item on his bucket list was to become a singer, but to his dismay he found that he couldn't carry a tune in a bucket.

Rejected line from *Gone with the Wind* draft script: "Frankly, my dear, I don't give a rat's patootie."

GAME SHOW HOST: "Name a famous singer."
CONTESTANT: "That's easy — my grandmother's Singer Sewing Machine."

He has a lot of class — but it's all low.

Never go hunting with a man named Chug-a-Lug.

RICK'S JOKE OF BOOKS II

LIFE HACK FOR HUSBANDS:
If your wife tries a new recipe for dinner, it probably won't go over too well if you look at the food and say, "What's this sh*t?"

Telling nun jokes can become addicting, a bad habit.

PHLEBOTOMIST: "You have good veins."
ME: "Great. At least there's one thing about me that isn't totally lousy."

Q: What do you call a vampire who officiates at baseball games?
A: A Vumpire.

I'm looking forward to the soon-to-be-released caveman police action film, *Cromagnum Force.*

By RICK

"So Sadie sez to me, she sez, that the postman, the milkman, the TV repairman, AND the pool boy were all hiding under the bed at the same time, and that clueless nitwit husband of hers didn't suspect a THING!"

RICK'S JOKE OF BOOKS II

Nosferatu Claus.

By RICK

ABOARD A TRAIN:
DRUNK: "Hey, lady, izzat yer kid or a chimpanzee? Haw-Haw!"
LADY: "How DARE you insult my son like that, you-you stew bum!"
CONDUCTOR: "Is there a problem here?"
LADY: "Yes! This inebriated person is being very insulting!"
CONDUCTOR: "Our sincere apologies, madam. We'll move you to the First Class car immediately. By the way, would your pet chimp like a banana?"

Q: What do you call it when a stripper is attacked by a vicious dog?
A: A strip maul.

Beware of the Dictator of the Alaskan wilderness — Mooseolini.

RICK'S JOKE OF BOOKS II

SUPERMAN™ LEARNING TO TYPE #1:
"The quick brown fox jumped over the lazy dog in a single bound."

SUPERMAN™ LEARNING TO TYPE #2:
"Now is the time for all good supermen to come to the aid of their country with powers and abilities far beyond those of mortal men."

Joining a Southern Batist church, Batman™ then got Batized.

Q: What's the favorite retirement town for cowboy book authors?
A: Tomestone, Arizona.

The favorite sport of acrobatic stamp collectors: Gymstampstics.

By RICK

REPORTER: "To what do you attribute your long life, sir?"
111-YEAR-OLD MAN: "To the fact that I haven't died yet."

If I knew I was going to live this long, I'd have taken better care of myself.

You know you're old when you do a Ben Turpin impression and nobody has any idea who he was.

You know you're an old man when a young woman tries flirting with you, and you say, "You're waving sugar under the nose of a dead horse."

Ancient Rome's most successful and prosperous emperor: Lucky Charmsius.

RICK'S JOKE OF BOOKS II

The two Bartlett Pears took up figure skating, formed a partnership, trained long and hard, and developed into a great Pears skating team.

Tape two utility knife blades to the tips of your index and middle fingers, grab and set down an ice cube, and you, too, can become a Finger Skater.

The two constantly arguing private detectives became known as the Bickering Dickering Private Dicks.

The bodybuilder rested so long between sets that his training method became known as Wait Training.

By RICK

A lousy joke is good for what ails you. A book full of them is a miracle cure. Or not.

No one had a clue that the mild-mannered plumber was actually the great super-hero, The Flush, who, with his sidekick Plumber's Helper, could unplug a clogged toilet or sink faster than a speeding bullet.

Entering the Fowl Olympics, the barnyard chicken sprinter proved it was faster than a speeding pullet. Much later, the chicken wrote its memoirs, which garnered it the coveted Pulletzer Prize.

Combining figure skating with The Big Top yields a Three-Rink Circus.

RICK'S JOKE OF BOOKS II

Her bridal veil was rather more substantial than typical ones, as it was a gift from her father, a beekeeper.

Today's the birthday of that famous corn magnate, Kernel Sanders.

Any time I receive an email with "Good Day" in the subject line, I know it's foreign spam.

You know you're a man who's getting old when you suddenly realize that 25-year-old women were born in 1999 (at this writing in 2024).

Dodging the lawnmower just barely, the bird narrowly escaped becoming Shredded Tweet.

By RICK

Be vigilant while typing. Transposing two letters changes "The Big Rock Candy Mountain" into "The Big Cock Randy Mountain." Moving a space one character to the left changes "She's at it again" to "She's a tit again." And "Regards" can become "Retards," while the old tractor company name "Cockshutt" can easily become something else.

Retiring from military conquest to become a writer of lousy joke books, Attila the Hun became known as Attila the Pun.

Attila also took up, as hobbies, bread-baking and beekeeping, thus gaining the nicknames Attila the Bun and Attila the Honey.

RICK'S JOKE OF BOOKS II

THE SCENE: A MAGICIAN PRODUCES A SMALL BLUE SILK OUT OF THIN AIR; THE SILK IS QUITE WRINKLED:
FEMALE SPECTATOR: "My, that silk is sure wrinkled."
MAGICIAN: "Yes. Almost as much as your face is. Haw-Haw!"

"Bark-Bark-Bark! Whine!"
"What's that, Classie? Timmy's trapped in a lousy-jokes book?"

The pirate was diligent in saving and investing his plunder. His name was Ness Tegg.

A pastor I once knew said that we can't drag the past into the present. In my case, it's not for lack of trying.

By RICK

I've heard many radio commercials by investment companies that state along the lines of, "If you have at least $50,000 to invest, send for our free report." What they're really saying is that "If you have less than $50,000 to invest, you're a peon and not worth two cents to us, so don't bother us."

When your food's running low five days before your next paycheck arrives, you WILL use honey with an expiration date of March 2004.

I've come across the term "Hot-Linking" of late. I assume it refers to some special method of cooking sausages, or some trendy new dating practice.

RICK'S JOKE OF BOOKS II

I never bother telling anyone that I'm normal. I'd feel too guilty over uttering such a big lie.

You know you're getting old when the only person who calls you a "young man" is a ninety-something lady.

You're getting old when you think a "Hashtag" is a receipt you'd receive in a greasy spoon — and when you remember the term "greasy spoon."

The favorite cleaning product of weightlifters: Mr. Clean & Jerk.

He tried to shoo away the bird, but it was unflappable.

By RICK

If you think you're delusional, but aren't, or think you're not delusional, but are, are you delusional or are you not?

You can be a child for only a short time, but you can be immature for your entire life. (Trust me on this.)

The Freemasons and the Knights Templar, flying space-worthy Black Helicopters, lifted off from a secret Lemurian base inside Mount Shasta, flew to Mars, and carved The Face On Mars with high-powered laser beams. The Truth is Out There. (Way Out There.)

Thanks to arthritis, I'm the gimp that keeps on gimping.

RICK'S JOKE OF BOOKS II

In a local grocery store, I saw that they were selling tubs of "Loaded Mashed Potatoes." I didn't buy any, however, as I prefer my mashed potatoes to be sober. If you've ever observed a plate of mashed potatoes singing "How Dry I Am," then you'll understand my position.

Two briskets got into an angry shouting match, a real beef.

While many traditional companies offer Live Chat, ghost companies offer Dead Chat.

We need a holiday or special occasion called "Belated." Then we could say "Happy Belated" with no guilt.

By RICK

DREAM: I died and went to Heaven. There, I watched as various people received the Crowns they had earned in life — the Crown of Righteousness, the Crown of Life, etc. Presently, an angel walked up to me and said sadly, "I'm sorry, Rick, but you didn't earn any Crowns. But here's your Participation Trophy."

HE: "Hey, Sweetcakes, where ya been all of my life?"

SHE: "Well for most of your life I wasn't even born yet."

Some look fondly back upon their high school days. All I can look back upon is my hi skool daze.

King Tutankhamun's lesser known brother: Tutuncommon.

RICK'S JOKE OF BOOKS II

I received a spam e-mail with this subject line: "Get the Hurricane Spin Broom Today." But I don't want to get the Hurricane Spin Broom today, or any other day. But if anyone reading this wants to get the Hurricane Spin Broom today (or any other day), then far be it from me to discourage you from acquiring said Hurricane Spin Broom today (or any other day you choose). Likewise, if anyone reading this doesn't want to get the Hurricane Spin Broom today (or any other day), then you are certainly under no obligation to acquire the Hurricane Spin Broom today (or any other day). So please don't fret over Hurricane Spin Broom acquisition or non-acquisition, whatever the case may be.

By RICK

DEVOTED FAN OF CELEBRITY: "Hi! I just won this great autographed photo of you in an online auction!"

CELEBRITY: "I'm very sorry, but that's not my signature. It's fake."

DEVOTED FAN: "But...It CAN'T be fake! It came with a Certificate of AUTHENTICITY!"

Sometimes it's best to walk away from a person or situation forever. Sometimes it's even better to leave a joke in your wake as you walk away from a person or situation forever.

She was a trophy wife, but her reputation was tarnished.

When you're lost, the Big Dipper and Summer Triangle are great navigational aids, unless it's mid-day.

The airport official was nonplussed to learn that there were no coat hangers in the hangars.

It is said that with age comes wisdom. In my case, all that's come with age is wisdumb.

SONG IN MY HEAD UPON AWAKENING ON THANKSGIVING DAY IN 2020: "Jack Frost roasting on an open fire. Chestnuts nipping at your nose..."

Still attending church and working as a veterinarian at his advanced age, the curmudgeon was a centenarian Presbyterian contrarian veterinarian.

Lumber salespersons must be Board Certified.

By RICK

IDEA: Why don't we shut down ALL brick-and-mortar businesses worldwide and replace them with one super-giant continent-sized Amazon®-type of online store? We could then have chips implanted in our skulls, all connected 24/7/365 to the super-giant online store. Thus equipped, all we'd have to do is say, for example, "Tea, Earl Grey, hot" or "Toilet paper, Two-Ply, Mega Rolls," and magically and quickly delivered at our front doors, via high-speed drones, would be steaming mugs of Earl Grey tea or mega rolls of two-ply toilet paper. We wouldn't even have to bestir ourselves from our chairs, or log onto any devices, for such to occur.

RICK'S JOKE OF BOOKS II

Why haven't we been contacted by, or made first contact with, extraterrestrials? Maybe it's because the insects on worlds with highly advanced space-faring civilizations are more advanced than humanity, and such civilizations thus consider us too insignificant to bother with. After all, offhand I can't think of anyone who's ever tried to strike up a conversation with a flea.

Q: What's the favorite deli sandwich among pro wrestlers?
A: The Hulk Hoagie.

Other than spring, summer, fall, and winter, I enjoy all the seasons.

By RICK

I glanced at a box of Rotini and noted that it's made with 100% Durum Wheat. This got me to thinking: Would Rotini made with 75% Durum Wheat and 25% Non-Durum Wheat be just as good, or nearly so? What about 50% Durum Wheat-50% Non-Durum Wheat Rotini, or 25% Durum Wheat-75% Non-Durum Wheat Rotini? And would 0% Durum Wheat-100% Non-Durum Wheat Rotini be serviceable, despite the complete absence of Durum Wheat? I can only conclude that the issue of Rotini vis-a-vis Durum Wheat content warrants further investigation and research on my part.

RICK'S JOKE OF BOOKS II

The Lousy Joke Book Writers of America (LJBWA) membership just graded all of my "A" material with an "F". I don't understand this, as I'm the LJBWA's only member. In any event, I must say that this distressing turn of events has left me positively HOUSEBROKEN.

Slipping on the icy sidewalk and taking a bad fall, Sigmund Freud was thereafter nicknamed Freudian Slip.

The mediocre figure skater retired from the sport, became a lawyer, and enjoyed much greater success as a slip-and-fall attorney.

King Tutankhamun's trumpet-playing brother: Tootin'-khamun.

By RICK

Q: What's the favorite gymnastics event among vegetarian gymnasts?
A: The Balance Bean.

All birds can talk. After all, talk is cheep.

I don't have a FICO® Score; I have a FAKE-O Score.

The spiciest time travel film: "The Thyme Machine."

Roy G. Biv is one colorful character.

Q: What's the favorite brand of walking shoes among chemists?
A: New Valence.

His mother being a witch made him a sonuva witch.

RICK'S JOKE OF BOOKS II

Q: Where do you find elephants?
A: It depends on where you lost them.

Q: What day of the week does Humpty Dumpty dread?
A: Fried-egg.

The pirate mechanic was upset over losing his favorite tool, his Crescent Wench.

If stored past its expiration date, does Egg Foo Young become Egg Too Old?

Nature, the family's dog, was terrified of their vacuum cleaner. Not surprising, since nature abhors a vacuum.

By RICK

GUY AND GAL IN A RESTAURANT, PERUSING THE MENU:
HE: "So, what do you think you'd like to have?"
SHE: "I feel like a plate of spaghetti with meatballs."
HE: "That's funny, you don't look like one."
SHE: "Har de Har Har."

They decided against installing siding on their home, the prohibitive cost of doing so being the de-siding factor.

Q: What do you call an underage elephant lawbreaker?
A: A Juvenelephant Delinquent.

RICK'S JOKE OF BOOKS II

Relocating from Wall Street to Stonehenge after joining the Druids, the successful hedge fund manager continued her career as a henge fund manager.

What were Sir Isacc Newton's favorite cookies?
A: Fig Newtons™, of course.

Dracula opened his own insurance company, All Stake, with the company motto: "You can count on the Count. You're in dead hands with All Stake."

The zombie insurance agent specialized in selling death insurance.

By RICK

I saw a sad clown recently. He was really clown in the dumps.

In the hot dog vending industry there are both losers and wieners.

Across the street from me lives a champion bodybuilder, Artie Biggerneighbor.

Little known is that there was a secret-agent Koi fish employed in the 00 Section of the British Secret Service. He always introduced himself by saying, "My name is Pond, James Pond."

Abandoning his life of evil, the terrorist took up fortune telling and became a Tarotist.

RICK'S JOKE OF BOOKS II

On my tombstone, I want chiseled the same wording as that displayed on lottery ticket readers in stores: "Sorry Not A Winner."

"I'm very sorry, Mister Bond, but we're all out of liquor. So what may we serve you instead?"
"One glass of water, please, shaken, not stirred."

I got fired from my job at a hot dog stand because I just couldn't cut the mustard and was always playing ketchup. But it's just as well because I really didn't relish that job.

The banana became a gymnast, known for her Banana Splits.

By RICK

On the first day of summer and winter each year, his arthritis is particularly painful, requiring him to apply a Solstice Poultice.

He moved his suncatcher away from the sunlight into a shady spot so that the sun wouldn't deteriorate it; but now he can't figure out why the suncatcher no longer works.

For the most part he likes his elevator shoes, except that he keeps tripping and falling on the 13th Floor.

Earning a Ph.D. in Applied Mathematics, the parrot was a well-educated polymath.

RICK'S JOKE OF BOOKS II

Although a milquetoast, the mathematician was renowned for his ability to solve deferential equations.

Never once has my vintage manual typewriter ever flashed "Loading…," "Not Responding," or "404 File Not Found."

I don't trust Cloud computing and data storage. After all, clouds do evaporate.

POST-PROSTATECTOMY DREAM:
TRIBAL CHIEFTAIN'S BEAUTIFUL DAUGHTER: "I shall bear you many strong sons!"
ME: "Sorry, but not without my prostate you won't."

By RICK

MODERN CLICHÉS (2024):
- "Bro be like…"
- "Deep dive into…"
- "Down the rabbit hole."
- "Every. Single. Time."
- "Game changer."
- "Health issue" (formerly "medical emergency" / "health crisis").
- "…Said no one ever."
- "Word salad."

Q: What do you call a headache that travels from one part of one's head to another?
A: A Migrate Headache.

Q: What are the opening lyrics to Dracula's favorite song?
A: "I want a ghoul, just like the ghoul that married dear old Vlad."

RICK'S JOKE OF BOOKS II

Once a standup comedian known for his deadpan delivery, he became a hospital-supplies delivery driver known for his bedpan deliveries.

Q: What do you call a zombie with incontinence?
A: Bed Pan Walking.

The mermaid worked as a long haul trucker, until the day her big rig hit an icy patch on the highway and fishtailed out of control.

Q: What do you call a singing octopus?
A: An Octavepus.

There's a new line of pants just for dogs: Bowser Trousers.

By RICK

Q: What's the favorite form of exercise among misers?
A: Tai Cheap.

Q: What's the favorite song among Ear, Nose & Throat doctors?
A: "Sweet Adenoid."

Q: How do moose greet one another on December 25th?
A: "Merry Christmoose!"

Doc: "So how are you today, sir?"
Patient: "Pretty good, doctor."
Doc: "Great. Next patient, please!"

The cut-rate gastroenterologist specialized in semicolonoscopies.

RICK'S JOKE OF BOOKS II

They should develop an OTC pain medication to treat Life-aches.

Mrs. O'Leary's cow kicking over a lantern and causing The Great Chicago Fire of 1871 is a perfect example of Cows and Effect.

Flat Earthers don't believe in Planet Earth; they believe in Platter Earth.

Q: How can you tell when an eel is high on drugs?
A: When it starts singing "Loose Eel in the Sky with Diamonds."

Give a man a fish and you'll feed him for a day. Teach a man to fish and he'll have to buy an expensive fishing license.

By RICK

I'm enjoying the new book series about the drunken wizard, Harry Potted.

Giving up his criminal career as a notorious lock-picker and safe-cracker to become a Gospel chorale singer, he went from being Mugsy The Wire to Mugsy The Choir.

Losing his temper and hurling flapjacks at his hapless assistant cook, the chef was arrested for Pancake Battery.

Being the first person surgically implanted with a bionic bladder, he became Bladdery Powered.

RICK'S JOKE OF BOOKS II

English writer William Penn had a cousin, also an author but almost unknown today — William Pencil.

Virtually unknown today is Salvador Dali's salad-making brother, Saladbar Deli.

Sadly, in being cooked and processed, the strawberries perished during the jam session.

Q: What's the favorite outdoor game among cadavers?
A: Formaldehyde-and-Seek.

Q: What's The Man In The Moon's favorite food?
A: Crescent Rolls.

By RICK

Using gene-splicing, the scientists created a Duck Billed Platypus/Golden Retriever hybrid — the world's first Platypooch.

Why are there six-packs when there are seven days in a week?

He was obsessed with developing and maintaining his six-pack abs, to the exclusion of everything and everyone else. But at least, even in a crunch, he had core values.

"Frankfurter, my dear, I don't give a damn."
   —Rhett Butler III, Hotdog Vendor

The tree surgeon made good money, but he had to quit because he couldn't stand the sight of sap.

RICK'S JOKE OF BOOKS II

Always carrying around a broom and a dustpan, the fastidious seal became known as The Good Housekeeping Seal, and was featured in an article in *The Walrus Journal*.

Performing countless pushups in the barnyard, the cow developed impressive Tri-tips.

The pie baker carried so many heavy trays of pies each day that he developed bulging muscular Piceps.

Having imbibed liberally of adult beverages, the trappers in the woods decided to play Musical Snares.

By RICK

Q: What's a great way to confuse an Olympic figure skater?
A: Put her in a round rink and tell her there's a gold medal in the corner.

I think it would be more logical and convenient if the seven days of the week were renamed thus: Oneday, Twoday, Threeday, Fourday, Fiveday, Sixday, Sevenday.

The gastroenterologist with very low self-esteem branched out into standup comedy, specializing in self-defeating humor.

The world is going to hand in a hellbasket.

RICK'S JOKE OF BOOKS II

In bringing the Universe into existence, God created everything from nothing. In bringing me into existence, God created nothing from nothing.

You know you're rather less than popular when, at your approach, people say, "Well here comes old Waste-O-Space."

You know you don't belong in a church when they excommunicate you, and you're just a first-time visitor there.

The Octopus population has its own version of the Bible, comprising the Old and New Tentacles, and including the Tentateuch.

By RICK

PHONE CONVERSATION:
INSURANCE AGENT: "Thanks for renewing your auto policy. By the way, do you have a pet?"
CUSTOMER: "Yes, I have a dog."
INSURANCE AGENT: "Would you like to buy insurance for your dog?"
CUSTOMER: "No, thanks. He doesn't drive anymore."

The more you study, the more you know. The more you know, the more you forget. The more you forget, the less you know. So why study?

The dogs enjoyed rolling in the grass for hours on end. They were, of course, Fescue dogs.

RICK'S JOKE OF BOOKS II

I find most websites irritating these days. When they ask me for my "Cookie Preferences," I always check the "Oatmeal Raisin Cookies" box but they keep sending me Peanut Butter cookies.

Famous tire brand names are often company Treadmarks.

After a successful 40-year career, the tire company CEO decided to retire. Later the company asked him to return, but he declined, having no desire to be a retread.

Combining physics with philosophy allowed Einstein to develop his famous Theory of Moral Relativityism.

By RICK

Accidentally banging his head hard against the open cabinet door, he uttered a string of vile concuss words.

Upon being delivered a badly torn and dented package, looking as if it had been dropped from a 20-story building, he realized it had been Dropped Shipped.

Winning the World Championship in his division, the powerlifter answered the questions of assembled reporters at a bench press conference.

You know you're getting old when an increasing number of your body parts end up in medical waste bags.

RICK'S JOKE OF BOOKS II

Q: What's brown and sounds like a bell?
A: Dung!

Q: What sound is produced when a dog rings a doorbell?
A: Ding-Dog.

Q: Why does New Jersey have the most toxic waste dumps while California has the most politicians?
A: Because New Jersey got first pick.

WISDOM FROM KING NEPTUNE: "Keep your friends close, and your anemones closer."

Q: What is a camel?
A: It's a mouse designed by a committee.

By RICK

No sooner had he entered the classroom when the sex therapist realized, to his great dismay, that he had misread the course catalog and had actually registered for an art course titled Master Painting.

SHE: "I'm sorry, but that was a really lousy joke."
ME: "Oh, don't I KNOW it!"

THE GREAT POLITICAL JOKE: "We're from the government and we're here to help."

THE GREAT COSMIC JOKE: If the human race renders itself extinct, via a full-scale nuclear World War III or some other calamity, the Cosmos won't even blink.

RICK'S JOKE OF BOOKS II

Those who die and go to Heaven will be surprised at who they see there. Those who die and go to Hell will be surprised at who they see there.

For some, Earth will be the only Hell they will ever know. For others, Earth will be the only Heaven they will ever know.

How ironic that I have depression but my blood type is B-Positive.

"Time is the fire in which we burn."
— Delmore Schwartz,
"Calmly We Walk Through
This April's Day," 1937

"Is it just me, or is it getting hotter in here?"
—Me, 2024

By RICK

Other than Sunday through Saturday, I enjoy every day of the week.

MAGIC SHOW CARD TRICK CLIMAX:
MAGICIAN: "And now, madam, please tell me and the audience the name of your selected card."
DUMB DORA: "I didn't look at it. Was I supposed to?"

I'm too young to die. I'm too ME to die.

After I die, I wonder how much of my life will end up in dump bags tossed carelessly in a dumpster.

Thought upon awakening in the middle of the night: I'll miss me when I die.

RICK'S JOKE OF BOOKS II

THE LAST JOKE

A visitor to the small coal mining town was sitting in the town's only bar one night, his first time there, when he noticed a man sitting off by himself, quietly nursing a beer. To the visitor's shock, he immediately noticed that the man's head was totally flat on the top and on the right side of his face, looking like half a box.

"What on earth happened to that guy?" the visitor asked the bartender, in a near-whisper.

"Oh, that's Mulligan. Long-time miner around these parts, and a big hero, too. Last year, he and several other miners were workin' down in the mine's deepest tunnel, when one of the support beams runnin' across the tunnel's ceiling began to crack and threatened to give way. If that'd

By RICK

happened, the entire ceiling could've collapsed right then and there, buryin' and killin' 'em all.

"But Mulligan stood under the beam and supported the weight of the entire ceiling on his head for minutes, long enough so's the other miners could temporarily shore up the ceiling with wood columns. That gave 'em all just enough time to escape before the entire ceiling came crashin' down.

"And that's how the top of his head got flat."

"Wow, that's an incredible story. But tell me: How did the right side of his face get flat?"

"Oh, that happened when the other miners grabbed him and sledge-hammered him into place."

RICK'S JOKE OF BOOKS II

MORE LOUSY STUFF

By RICK

RICK'S JOKE OF BOOKS II

RECENT NEWS HEADLINES

- "Mr. Peanut™ Diagnosed with Planters Fasciitis."
- "Patina's Reputation Tarnished."
- "Percale Three Sheets to the Wind, Arrested for DUI."
- "Pandora Wins Boxing Title."
- "Cleopatra Uses Sharpie® Pen to Marc Antony."
- "Roy Rogers' Horse Begins Trigger Point Therapy."
- "The Society of Time Travelers to Hold its Next Annual Meeting Last Tuesday at Noon."

*****

By RICK

RICK'S JOKE OF BOOKS II

A MARTIAL ARTS GLOSSARY OF THE MARTIAL ARTS

Aikeydo: The classic martial art of preference among locksmiths.

Eyekido: The classic martial art of preference among eye doctors.

Jaw-Jitsu: The classic martial art most popular among dentists. (Recommended by four out of five dentists surveyed.)

Jew-Jitsu: The classic martial art most popular among Rabbis.

Karate-Dough: The much-kneaded martial art.

Kendon't: The martial art of inept swordspersons.

By RICK

Marital Arts: Secret and enigmatic arts mastered only by the fortunate few living in wedded bliss.

Qigong: The ancient health practice that's best for those who are all keyed up.

Tae Kwon Dough: The ancient martial art of breaking bread.

Tai Cheese: The ancient health-promoting martial art favored by those in the dairy industry.

Termité: The ancient martial art of Biting Wood.

Tie Chi: The ancient health-promoting martial art for the straight-laced who know the ropes and are knotty by nature.

* * * * *

RICK'S JOKE OF BOOKS II

POETRY CORNER

HEAD BUMP

I bumped my head.
I should be dead.
It's off to bed.

* * * * *

AREN'T YOU GLAD?[1]

I'm glad I use Dial.
As proof here's my wrapper.
The soap's in the soap dish.
Right next to my crapper.

* * * * *

---

[1] Decades ago the makers of Dial Soap™ ran a contest in which people could mail in new advertising slogans for the product. This was my father's entry. Sadly, my mother forbade him from sending it.

By RICK

HUMPTY DUMPSTER

Humpty Dumpty sat on a wall.
Humpty Dumpty had a great fall.
All the king's horses and
All the king's men
Tossed his remains in a
Humpty dumpster.

* * * * *

HUMPTY DUMPNOG

Humpty Dumpty sat on a wall.
Humpty Dumpty had a great fall.
All the king's horses and
All the king's men
Used him to mix up a batch of
Egg Nog.

* * * * *

RICK'S JOKE OF BOOKS II

GIRL FROM INSTITUTE[2]

A Rootity Toot!
A Rootity Toot!
I'm a girl from Institute!
I don't smoke,
And I don't chew,
And I don't go with
Boys who do!

* * * * *

CHRISTMAS POEM

Kris Kringle
Is single
And on his roof are shingles
And on his sleigh are bells that jingle.
Kringle single shingle jingle.

* * * * *

---

[2] A century ago my mother's father, Royal, liked to recite this rhyme while doing a silly little dance in front of her and her younger sister, Marge, when they were children. I don't know the rhyme's origin.

By RICK

RICK'S JOKE OF BOOKS II

BABOON: A TRUE STORY

A coworker of mine back in the day, Nana was an exotically beautiful woman with a long, porcelain face and high cheekbones.

One day, Nana showed up at work sporting a significant quantity of peach-colored rouge on her cheeks. Seeing her in this configuration, I realized with a start that the thick rouge on her high cheekbones, combined with her usual bright-red lipstick, gave her rather more than a passing resemblance to a baboon.

We were talking in the company break room when this realization struck me abruptly, and it was all I could do to stifle a paroxysm of laughter, which I did via a fake coughing spell.

By RICK

Thereafter, Nana continued using that rouge. Although I tried with all my willpower, I could no longer be anywhere near her without *BABOON! BABOON! BABOON! BABOON! BA-BA-BABOON! VA-VA-VA-VOOM!* pounding through my brain.

I still regarded her as a beautiful woman, but now with an impossible-to-ignore air of baboonishness about her.

I must mention that this was entirely my fault, and not Nana's in the slightest. Sadly, throughout my life, my brain has had the tendency to obsessively latch onto ideas, often crazy ones, and not let go of them.

Once, I awoke in the middle of the night to these song lyrics playing in my brain: *"Up, up and away, with my beautiful baboon."*

On another night, I dreamed about Nana and I getting married. In my dream I was standing next to her, in front of the preacher, thinking, *I can't believe this! I'm about to marry a woman who looks like a baboon! I must have gone bananas!* In reality, however, romance, much less marriage, was never remotely possible for us — not because I had any aversion to exotically beautiful women, even those with baboonish tendencies, but because our personalities were simply not compatible and we had little in common.

Plus, I'm admittedly quite plain in appearance, and "available" women have invariably found me about as attractive as a pile of dog doo.

Nana had a kind heart, but it was buried beneath a proud and temperamental personality; she was quick to anger and to hold a grudge. Consequently, I never dared mention to

By RICK

her that I thought she looked like a baboon — albeit a beautiful one. Had I done so, she would most certainly have gone totally ape.

But even had I wanted to, how could I have told Nana of her baboon resemblance in a way that wouldn't have offended her? After all, how DO you tell a woman in a nice and tactful way that she looks like a baboon?

I suppose I could have used the direct approach: "I've been meaning to tell you something *really* interesting: Did you know that you look like a baboon?" But all that would have gotten me are a tongue lashing and likely a smack or three in the face.

Or I could have tried the indirect approach: "Have you ever noticed that baboons look a lot like women who've applied lots of rouge to their cheeks?

Oh, by the way..." But that wouldn't have cut it either.

Of course, I could have opted for the subtle approach: "I just think that baboons are *sooo* cute. And you know what? I think that you're cute in much the same way." Nope. Forget that, too.

I guess that in some situations silence is golden after all.

If there's a lesson in this tale (tail?), it is this: Ladies, if you're beautiful with a long face and high cheekbones, or even if you're not, go easy on the rouge. Unless, that is, you're trying to woo Tarzan, King Kong, or Mighty Joe Young.

~Th-Th-Th-That's All Folks!~

APPENDIX

TESTIMOANIALS AND PREYS FROM READERS

Remainder table fodder — both the book and the author.
—B.A. Noble

Rick thinks I look like a WHAT?!?
—Nana

Arr! There be lousy joke books here, I trow! Arr-Arr-Arr!
—Satisfied Pirate

I think, therefore I wish I had neither read this book nor heard of the author.
—R. Descartes

It's patently obviously that liberal quantities of adult beverages fueled the writing of this.
—O. John Barleycorn

Jeepers! This is swell!
—Jimmy O.

Tea Hee.
—Earl Grey

Angels and ministers of grace defend us from these sordid bon mots!

—Bard Shaxberd

The author needs to quit writing while he's still behind.

—Writing Coach

The book is full of reports on different secret ways to beat up people.

—Gilbey J. Amry

Never mind Time. Lousy Jokes are the fire in which this author burns.

—Delmore S.

Someone's going to find a nice big lump of coal in his Christmas stocking this year, someone is.

—St. Nick

Never have I HO-HO-HOed so little-little-little in my life-life-life!

—S. Claus

Aye-Aye! 'Allo-'Allo-'Allo! What's all THIS, then?

—Bobby Copper

A joke book? I thought I was buying a yolk book. At any rate, this thing's a literary dumpster fire. I regret having wasted the money I shelled out for it.
—Humpty Dumpster

Do not go gentle into this bad blight. Rage, rage against the writing of such tripe.
—Dylan T.

You blockhead author Rick!
—L. van Pelt

You're not doing a really good job.
—Kim Y., Retired Figure Skater

This thing reduced my Kindle™ to kindling!
—E. Bookie

By hook or by crook this shall stay off my Nook™.
—E. Pubb

Of all the bookshelves in all the towns in all the world, and this author's joke books had to show up on mine.
—Rick (no relation)

Holy lousiest joke book I've ever read!
—D. Grayson

Well here's ANOTHER nice collection of lousy jokes you've gotten me into!

—Ollie H.

Fee-fi-fo-fum, I smell the blood of a joking bum!

—A. Giant

One lousy joke book, please, shaken, not stirred.

—J. Bond

Never have I encountered so egregious an example of joke apostasy.

—J. Calvin

* HIC *

—A. Capp

* HIC *

—Baba Rum Dum

And the author and his lousy jokes were dead before they hit the floor.

—1970s Kung-Fu Novel Writer

Yarf-Yarf.

—Pat B.

ABOUT RICK
(WHO HE?)

Following thrilling stints as a slapstick film comedian at the Hal Cockroach Studios, a temp sailor through the Gobs-R-Us Temporary Employment Agency, a spinach wholesaler, a Zamboni mechanic, a banana ripening room supervisor, a Duck-Billed Platypus Tamer and Elephant Cage Sanitary Engineer in the Ding-a-ling Brothers Circus, an anointed Tuna Casserole Taste Tester for the Southern Baptist Convention, a chiropractor trained at the renowned Sorebone University, a hot chocolate lush, a figure skating dress designer, a porta-potty maintenance truck operator for Any Old Porta-Potty In The Storm Inc., a male cake-popper through his Limited Liability Corporation You Can Have Your Cake And Eat It Too LLC, a freelance Guy Friday on Mondays through Thursdays, and a book formatter and copy editor of marginal proficiency and no renown, Rick Helley turned his attention to compiling into book form his lousy jokes spanning decades. His first joke book, *RICK'S JOKE OF BOOKS*, and the present volume, *RICK'S JOKE OF BOOKS II*, are the result.

    Rick lives in San Jose, Calif., about which he thinks it could rightly be said, "There's No There There."

Rick & friends at The Flying Lady Restaurant, Morgan Hill, Calif., in 1991. Rick is the one with no hat.

Milton Keynes UK
Ingram Content Group UK Ltd.
UKHW020035271124
451585UK00012B/871